I0821214

Sun Bear

by Julie Murray

Abdo Kids Jumbo is an Imprint of Abdo Kids
abdobooks.com

abdobooks.com

Published by Abdo Kids, a division of ABDO, P.O. Box 398166, Minneapolis, Minnesota 55439.

Printed in the United States of America, North Mankato, Minnesota.

102024

012025

Photo Credits: Alamy, Getty Images, Minden Pictures, Shutterstock

Production Contributors: Teddy Borth, Jennie Forsberg, Grace Hansen
Design Contributors: Victoria Bates, Candice Keimig

Library of Congress Control Number: 2024936632

Publisher's Cataloging-in-Publication Data

Names: Murray, Julie, author.

Title: Sun bear / by Julie Murray

Description: Minneapolis, Minnesota : Abdo Kids, 2025 | Series: Unusual animals | Includes online resources and index.

Identifiers: ISBN 9798384903086 (lib. bdg.) | ISBN 9798384903789 (ebook) | ISBN 9798384904137 (Read-to-me ebook)

Subjects: LCSH: Sun bear--Juvenile literature. | Bears--Juvenile literature. | Nocturnal animals--Juvenile literature. | Rain forest animals--Juvenile literature. | Wildlife--Juvenile literature. | Enigmas--Juvenile literature.

Classification: DDC 599.78--dc23

Table of Contents

Sun Bear

The sun bear is the smallest bear **species**. It lives in Southeast Asia in wooded areas and tropical forests.

Asia
Sun Bear Range

Sun bears are unusual! They have a golden patch of fur on their chest. The fur looks like a rising sun. This is how the bear got its name.

Body

Sun bears can weigh up to 150 pounds (68 kg) and grow up to 4 feet (1.52 m) long. Their **stocky** bodies are covered with black fur.

Sun bears can walk on two or four legs. They have very good **balance** walking on two legs.

Sun bears have front feet that point inward. This **trait**, along with their curved claws and flat chest, allow them to be excellent climbers.

Sun bears spend much of the day up in trees. They sunbathe and rest on branches anywhere from 7 to 23 feet (2.1 m to 7 m) off the ground.

Food

Sun bears are **nocturnal**. They roam the forest at night in search of food. They like to eat fruit, insects, roots, and small animals.

But the sun bear's favorite food is honey! It uses its sharp claws to rip open beehives. Its extra-long tongue slurps out the honey.

Baby Sun Bears

Females give birth to one or two cubs at a time. Cubs are born hairless and helpless. They stay with their mother for about two years.

More Facts

- A sun bear's chest marking is like a fingerprint. No two bears have the same marking!
- The sun bear is a **vocal** bear. It clucks, barks, growls, and roars.
- It has the longest tongue of any bear **species**. The tongue can be up to 10 inches (24.4 cm) long!

Glossary

balance – the state of being steady in body.

nocturnal – active at night.

species – a group of living things that look alike and can have young together.

stocky – thick, sturdy, and often short in build.

trait – a characteristic or quality that makes an animal different from others.

vocal – having or exercising the power of producing voice or sound.

Index

Visit **abdokids.com** to access crafts, games, videos, and more!